Much Ado About Nothing

For Kids

by *Lois Burdett*

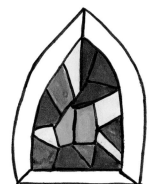

FIREFLY BOOKS

A FIREFLY BOOK

Published by Firefly Books Ltd. 2002

Publisher Cataloging-in-Publication Data (U.S.)

Burdett, Lois,
    Much ado about nothing for kids / Lois Burdett.—1st ed.
[64] p. : col. ill. ; cm. —(Shakespeare can be fun!)
Summary: Retelling of the classic play written in rhyming couplets. Writings and art by children help narrate the book.
ISBN 1-55209-411-1
ISBN 1-55209-413-8 (pbk.)
1. Shakespeare, William, 1564-1616—Adaptions. 2. Shakespeare, William, 1564-1616. Much ado about nothing. 3. Young adult drama, English. I. Shakespeare, William, 1564-1616. Much ado about nothing. II. Title. III. Series: Burdett, Lois. Shakespeare can be fun!.

822.3/ 3 21   CIP   PR2828.A2B87 2002

National Library of Canada Cataloguing in Publication Data

Burdett, Lois,
        Much ado about nothing for kids

(Shakespeare can be fun)
ISBN 1-55209-411-1 (bound).—ISBN 1-55209-413-8 (pbk.)

        1. Shakespeare, William, 1564-1616—Adaptations—Juvenile literature. 2. Readers' theatre. I. Shakespeare, William, 1564-1616. Much ado about nothing. II. Title. III. Series.

PR2878.M82B87 2002   jC812'.54   C2002-900229-X

Published in Canada in 2002 by
Firefly Books Ltd.
3680 Victoria Park Avenue
Willowdale, Ontario
Canada M2H 3K1

Published in the U.S. in 2002 by
Firefly Books (U.S.) Inc.
P.O. Box 1338, Ellicott Station
Buffalo, New York
14205, United States

Printed and bound in Canada
by Friesens, Altona, Manitoba

Design concept by Lois Burdett

We acknowledge the financial support of the Government of Canada through the Book Publishing Industry Development Program for our publishing activities.

Scott Wishart, The Beacon Herald

Matt Hunt (age 7)
Lois Burdett's Grade 2 students

Sophie Jones (age 7)

Foreword

I have long been an admirer of Shakespeare and his ability to tell a really great story. How many writers throughout time have been equally at ease writing tragedy, comedy and recreating a part of their nation's history? Once you open the door to Shakespeare there are so many wonderful discoveries just waiting to be made.

One of my favorite Shakespearean comedies is *Much Ado About Nothing,* a story about love, family, friendship and trust. This is a tale of romance and deception wrapped in a rich mantle of humor which captivates audiences today as surely as it did four hundred years ago. I had the pleasure of playing Don Pedro, Prince of Aragon, in a film version of this play and one thought that stood out in my mind was how well the characters stood the test of time.

Lois Burdett must be congratulated on her innovative approach to Shakespeare for younger audiences. Her delightfully entertaining text is complemented by her students' thoughtful interpretations and charming artwork which make *Much Ado About Nothing* come alive in a whole new way.

I hope you enjoy this book as much as I have and find Shakespeare as thrilling as I do.

DENZEL WASHINGTON

THE CHARACTERS

Citizens of Messina

LEONATO . . . . Governor of Messina
HERO . . . . Daughter of Leonato
BEATRICE . . . . Niece of Leonato
ANTONIO . . . . Brother of Leonato
FRIAR FRANCIS . . . . A priest
DOGBERRY . . . . Master Constable
VERGES . . . . Assistant to Dogberry
FIRST WATCHMAN ⎫
SECOND WATCHMAN ⎭ . . . . Officers of Dogberry
TOWN CLERK . . . . A notary for legal matters
MARGARET ⎫
URSULA ⎭ . . . . Gentlewomen attending on Hero

Visitors to Messina

DON PEDRO . . . . Prince of Aragon
DON JOHN . . . . Half-brother of Don Pedro
CLAUDIO . . . . A young lord of Florence
BENEDICK . . . . A young lord of Padua
BORACHIO ⎫
CONRADE ⎭ . . . . Followers of Don John

Others

MUSICIANS, PARTY AND WEDDING GUESTS
ATTENDANTS AND MESSENGERS

Mike Schmidt (age 10)

I have a story, with an all-star cast,
Set in Sicily, in times long past.
Beatrice and Benedick, the heroes of my play,
Battle with words and wit everyday.
But I have a plan to unite the two,
That is intended to entertain you.
So join me, my friends, under Messina's sky,
As Signior Benedick and his troop draw nigh.

These valiant soldiers were returning from war,
And all of Messina was in an uproar.
Everywhere excitement flared,
As entertainment was prepared.
Leonato, the governor of the town,
Was there to greet these men of renown.
Hero, his daughter, stood by his side,
The thrill in her heart could not be denied.
Beatrice, his niece, was also close by,
A look of pleasure sparkled in her eye.

Leonato   Hero   Beatrice

Eliza Johnson (age 9)

As sounds of approaching horses grew loud,
A rousing cheer echoed throughout the crowd.
Don Pedro, Prince of Aragon, was in the lead,
Riding proud on his dappled steed.
Benedick of Padua was the next they spied,
With Count Claudio of Florence by his side.
Don John, the Prince's brother, was the last to appear,
And with his attendants brought up the rear.
The Prince dismounted without delay,
"Leonato, do you come to greet trouble today?"
He gave the governor a hearty embrace,
Leonato smiled, "Not trouble, but comfort, Your Grace."

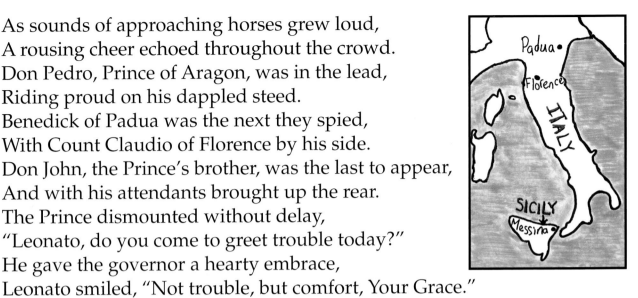

Map: Graeme Henry (age 8)
Picture: Katie Besworth (age 9)

"I think this is your daughter," said the Prince bowing low.
Leonato laughed, "Her mother hath many times told me so."
Benedick smirked, "Good sir, was there doubt in your mind?"
To Beatrice, this exchange was becoming unkind.
She thought Benedick was obnoxious and rude,
And disliked his behaviour and attitude.
"Still talking, Signior Benedick? No one listens to you!"
And a heated argument began to brew.
Whenever they met, these two struck the wrong chord,
And their stinging insults could not be ignored.
Benedick's remark was no less forgiving,
"What, my dear Lady Disdain! Are you yet living?"

Dear Beatrice,
Get a life! You think I blacken the day? When you speak, smiles turn to frowns. I have heard too many of your dull and foolish jokes. So quit your whining!
     Your worst nightmare,
              Benedick

Story: Madison Foster (age 7)
Picture: Jeremiah Courtney (age 9)

Benedick

8

"Is it possible," Beatrice sneered and let out a sigh,
"With Signior Benedick to mock, Disdain should die?"
Benedick bragged, "I am loved by all ladies, except one,
For truly," he continued, "I love none!"
Beatrice countered each insult, blow for blow,
"I had rather hear my dog bark at a crow
Than a man swear he loves me or be so inclined."
Benedick jeered, "Keep your ladyship in that frame of mind.
I would my horse had the speed of your tongue," he taunted.
"I know all your tricks," she replied, undaunted.
Don Pedro interrupted, "Leonato's asked us to stay.
We'll remain here at least a month from today."

Benedick, you annoying pest, your mouth blabs more than a parrot squacks. You're such a bragging show-off. If I wrote a book about famous people, you would be celebrated for your mouth. You're always muttering and sputtering about something.
Beatrice

Story: Lauri-Beth Lewis (age 7)
Picture: Katie Besworth (age 9)

Beatrice

9

Then to Leonato's, the royal group departed.
Claudio remained with Benedick, feeling light-hearted.
"My friend," Claudio exclaimed, his eyes aglow,
"Did you take note of Leonato's daughter, Hero?
She is the sweetest lady that ever I looked on," he sighed.
"I see no such matter," Signior Benedick cried.
"If her cousin Beatrice did not hold such rage,
She would outshine Hero on any stage.
Claudio, I think your mind's in a haze,
Hero's too short and tiny for such great praise.
Would you buy her my friend? Now, don't be a fool!"
Claudio sighed, "Can the world buy such a jewel?"

Dear Benedick,
Heaven has fallen upon my world. A song of love is locked in my mind and rings forth the name Hero. Her face is the dawning of day. Her eyes shimmer with the light of the moon. Swans, doves and even the sun are gifts to the earth, but to me it is Hero!
                    Claudio

Claudio

Story: Kelsey Cunningham (age 7)
Picture: Elly Vousden (age 8)

This lovesick behaviour put Benedick in a stew,
"I hope you have no intent to turn husband, have you?"
Claudio persisted, "I want Hero in my life!
I would marry, if she were to be my wife."
Benedick turned up his nose in disgust,
"Has it come to this? You should readjust.
Claudio, can't you see you are acting insane?
Shall I never see a bachelor of threescore again?"

Dear Claudio,
You have got to be kidding!
A soldier who wants to be married? I would rather be eaten by a piranha. Shape up! Knock some sense into your brain! Girls are just trouble!
                    Benedick

Story: Willie Malmo (age 7)
Picture: Ashley Kropf (age 10)

Benedick

11

Just then Don Pedro returned in dismay,
"What is the cause of your delay?
Why didn't you follow to Leonato's place?"
Benedick replied, "I will be candid, Your Grace.
Claudio's in love, the foolish man,
To marry Hero is his ludicrous plan."
"The lady is most worthy," Don Pedro replied.
Benedick rolled his eyes and continued to chide,
"You say she's worthy? I disagree!
And these feelings, fire cannot melt out of me."

Benedick

Don Pedro,
It's most certainly dastardly!!!
Claudio is in love with the
Governor's daughter, the little
shrimp. You and I both know a
woman can be very fickle. First
she'll toil with his mind, then
reject his feelings. A man his
age should watch out for
the grasping jaws of ladies!!
            The fuming Benedick

Story: Courtney Cunningham (age 8)
Picture: Jeremiah Courtney (age 9)

12

Don Pedro gave Benedick a playful shove,
"I shall see thee, before I die, look pale with love!"
"With anger, with sickness, or with hunger, my lord,"
Benedick began. "Not with love!" he roared.
Don Pedro chuckled, "These thoughts you'll revoke,
Then you'll be the target for many a joke."
"I will trust no woman," Benedick began,
"I shall always stay a single man!"
Then to Leonato's, Benedick took his leave,
To confirm their attendance at supper that eve.

Dear Benedick,
Don't be so sure. This is a stage most men go through. Someday I'll see you blush with a happy heart, your eyebrows curl and you will be head over heels in love. Trust me! You won't be a bachelor forever!
                              Don Pedro

Story: Elizabeth Farrell (age 7)
Picture: Valerie Sproat (age 11)

Don Pedro

Claudio turned to Don Pedro and implored,
"Hath Leonato any son, my lord?"
"No child but Hero. She's his only heir.
If you love her, Claudio, do not despair.
Cherish Hero, if your feelings are true.
Shall I talk with the lady and her father, too?"
"I'd welcome your help," Claudio replied,
"With my words she might be dissatisfied.
At courting, I believe you have more skill."
So the Prince offered a plan of his own free will.
"To make you the light in Hero's eyes,
I will assume thy part in some disguise,
And advise your lady, I am Claudio instead.
Then, with passion and flair, I'll ask her to wed.
When I win Hero's heart by my cunning design,
I'll speak with her father, then she shall be thine."

Dear Don Pedro,
In you there's a lover's mind. Exotic words blossom on your lips while I'm as tongue-tied as a lobster pinched in his own claws. Do men's hearts cry for a young lady like her? Yes! Yes, ever so sweetly. If you would win her for me I would be so grateful.
                    Claudio

Story: Kelsey Cunningham (age 8)
Picture: Lisa Hoeg (age 10)

Claudio

While Claudio wished good luck to his master,
There was another who craved Don Pedro's disaster.
This man so resentful, angry and withdrawn
Was the Prince's half-brother, the sullen Don John.
On opposite sides in the war they had fought,
Don John, the loser, was very distraught.
He despised the Prince, victorious in war,
And desperately wanted to settle the score.
Conrade, his follower, offered Don John advice,
"Conceal your feelings or you'll pay the price."
"I had rather be a canker in a hedge," Don John sneered,
"Than a rose in his grace to be revered!
I am a plain-dealing villain, so let me be!
I cannot hide what I am. Seek not to alter me."

Dear Conrade,
Don Pedro showers in the rain
of glory while a black cloud
hovers over my head. Any
hope of victory has been swept
away by my brother. He is a
proud rose and I am an ugly
weed. I will hide in the thicket
until I can plot my revenge!
                    Don John

Story: Joy McKeown (age 7)
Picture: Eliza Johnson (age 8)

Don John

As Don John paced and continued to fume,
Another of his followers entered the room.
Borachio announced, "I've overheard a secret plan
Of a possible marriage with your brother's right-hand man."
"The most exquisite Claudio?" Don John sneered in reply,
"Tell me Borachio, who has caught his eye?"
"Indeed, it is Hero, the Governor's daughter," he said,
"The Prince will act the lover so Claudio can be wed."
Don John snickered, "This information I can use,
It adds fuel to my desire. Now, Claudio may lose!
He took all the glory in the last campaign,
But I'll make sure his triumph has been totally in vain.
Come now, will you assist me?" Don John implored.
Conrade answered for them both, "To the death, my lord!"

Dear Don John,
I have astonishing news!
It might perk up that
gloomy face of yours.
Don Pedro is planning to
use his sweet words to
win the fair Hero for
Claudio. This is the
time for action!
            Borachio

Borachio

Story: Sam Johnson (age 7)
Picture: Julian Hacquebard (age 7)

16

Meanwhile, at Leonato's, a dance would soon commence.
For the guests' arrival, everyone waited in suspense.
"Was not Don John here at supper?" Leonato began.
Antonio, the governor's brother, said, "I didn't see the man."
Beatrice interrupted, "Don John always looks so sour!
I never can see him, but I am heart-burned for an hour."
Hero agreed, "To melancholy he's inclined."
Then Beatrice droned on about marriage and mankind.
"Don John's like a painted picture and says nothing at all.
Then there's Benedick whose chatter drives me up the wall.
Midway between these two is the perfect mate."
Leonato warned, "Niece, you'll never have a date.
With your sharp tongue, how can you hope to be a bride?"
"I never wish to marry!" she sternly replied,
"Each day I give my blessings that this remain the case.
With my luck, I'd get one with a beard on his face."

Dear Leonato and Hero,
I would not marry a man with
a beard if the whole universe
depended on it. I'd rather be
eaten by a Chinese dragon on
New Year's Eve.

Beatrice

Story: Max Besworth (age 7)
Picture: Valerie Sproat (age 11)

Then came the sound of fanfare and everyone cheered,
They all donned their masks as the revellers appeared.
While the music played, they paired up two by two,
Behind the disguises, no one knew who was who.
Don Pedro wooed Hero with loving words so sweet,
And proposed for Claudio so the deed would be complete.
Ursula, Hero's servant, was dancing to and fro
With Leonato's brother, the old Antonio.
And Margaret, another maid, was whisked off her feet
By an unknown fellow, who was swaying to the beat.

Elly Vousden (age 8)

18

Benedick standing near, watched this scene unfold,
Then he approached a lady in a manner bold.
It was his rival Beatrice hidden in disguise.
Behind their masks, they stared into each other's eyes.
To avoid detection he altered his speech,
And changed his tone into a high screech.
"I overheard a conversation," he began to wail,
"They say Beatrice is scorned and her jokes are stale."
"Will you not tell me who you are?" she implored.
"Not now!" Benedick replied, as his voice soared.
"And who told you that?" Beatrice continued in a huff,
"I'll bet it's Benedick! You know him well enough."

Eliza Johnson (age 8)

Benedick muttered, "You'll have to pardon me,
I do not know this man! Benedick? Who is he?"
"Why, he is the Prince's jester, a very dull fool,
His only skill is contriving slanders and ridicule."
Benedick burned with rage and felt his face turn red.
"If I meet him," he replied, "I'll tell him what you said."
"Do, do," Beatrice scoffed, "but I can foresee,
Benedick will counter with a joke about me."
Then Beatrice motioned him with a sideways glance,
"Come, we must follow the leaders of the dance."

Dear Masked Man,
Do you know Signior
Benedick? He is the Prince's
jester and a blabbering
fool. His jokes are as
rotten as mouldy cheese.
To get him to close his
mouth is like stopping
a wolf from howling.
Do you think he was
born on April Fools Day?
                    Beatrice

Story: Lauri-Beth Lewis (age 7)
Picture: Julie Wilhelm (age 10)

Meanwhile, Don Pedro had played Claudio's part,
And with eloquent words had won Hero's heart.
But Claudio knew nothing of this consequence,
As the dancers dispersed, he waited in suspense.
Don John and Borachio watched him pacing in a trance,
To avenge the Count, this was their perfect chance.
They approached Claudio, but called him Benedick.
"I'm worried," Don John lied, "The Prince is lovesick!
He's fallen for Hero but she's no equal for his birth."
Claudio's face grew pale and lost all its mirth.
"How do you know he loves her?" Claudio cried.
"I heard him vow he'd marry her," Borachio replied.
When the two departed, Claudio was enraged,
"Don Pedro courts for himself. I've been upstaged!
In affairs of love, no friend can be trusted!
Farewell, therefore, Hero!" In her, he was disgusted.

Dear Diary,
I have been betrayed by my buddy Don Pedro just when I least expected it. There is no doubt that he has robbed me of my heart's delight. Love has floated away like a hot balloon. As a friend Don Pedro is history! He's done me wrong!
Claudio

Story: William Wellington (age 7)
Picture: Cagney Schaeffer (age 9)

21

A few moments later, Signior Benedick arrived.
"Claudio, is that you? Your hopes are revived!
For the Prince hath got your Hero!" Benedick declared.
"I wish him joy with her!" Claudio glared.
"What's your problem?" Benedick asked in dismay,
"Do you think he has mistreated you some way?"
But the Prince's good deeds, the Count would not believe,
And in an angry frenzy, Claudio turned to leave.
"Poor hurt fowl!" said Benedick when he stood alone.
Then he thought of Beatrice, "Her words I can't condone!
I wonder if she knew it was me in disguise?
Did she speak in jest to ridicule and chastise?
Or was she unaware and meant the words she spoke?
Does she really think that I am such a joke?
The Prince's fool? Ha! I am not so reputed!
These are her bitter words and must be disputed."

Benedick

Thoughts of Benedick
How dare she insult me! Is this her idea of a joke or does she know it's me behind this mask? She speaks like a hyena. Well her tongue may be fast but mine is faster. I'll get her back for this.

Story: Willie Malmo (age 7)
Picture: Anika Johnson (age 9)

Just then the Prince appeared, "Hero's father has agreed.
I must tell Claudio, his wedding will proceed."
Benedick replied, "My friend thinks he's been deceived.
I told him she consented, but I was not believed."
Don Pedro interrupted, "Hero loves him true,
But the Lady Beatrice has a quarrel with you."
Benedick groaned, "Oh, she cannot be endured!
Beatrice speaks daggers and will never be cured.
She dared to call me the Prince's jester.
I tell you, Don Pedro, I really detest her!"
The Prince chuckled, "Here she comes, my friend."
Benedick exclaimed, "Command me to the world's end!"
The sight of Beatrice filled him with dread,
And with a hasty goodbye, Benedick quickly fled.

Don Pedro

Dear Don Pedro,
Beatrice is a thorn in my hand. I say one word and she snaps a thousand. She's like the raging rapids. Oh sire, here she comes. Banish me from this land. I'll find thee pearls from Tahiti, tea from China. Just get me out of here!
Benedick

Story: Joy McKeown (age 7)
Picture: Valerie Sproat (age 11)

Beatrice approached, with Claudio by the hand,
"I've brought the Count, as was your command."
Don Pedro inquired, "My friend, why are you sad?
What's wrong with you, Claudio? Are you sick, my lad?"
But this faulty notion, Beatrice tried to dispel,
"The Count is neither sad, nor sick, nor merry, nor well.
He's jealous and thinks you tricked him, my lord!"
"Claudio, your beliefs are false!" the Prince deplored.
"I have wooed in thy name and fair Hero is won,
Her father has consented. Now my job is done."
Then Leonato arrived with Hero by his side.
"Count Claudio, take my sweet daughter for your bride."
The young man was speechless and knew not what to do.
"Speak, Count!" urged Beatrice, "'Tis your cue!"
Claudio stammered, "Dear Hero, my heart soars."
He promised, "Lady, as you are mine, I am yours!"

Anika Johnson (age 10)

24

Beatrice prompted Hero, "Speak cousin, or, if you cannot,
Stop his mouth with a kiss. Give it your best shot!"
Any thoughts of betrayal they would now replace,
And soon the two were locked in a loving embrace.
Don Pedro chuckled, "Beatrice, you have a merry heart!"
Beatrice confided, "It keeps sorrow apart!
Everyone in the world has a mate but I.
Good Lord, send me a husband, by and by!"
The Prince interrupted with his own plea,
"I will get you one. How about me?"
"No, my lord, I was born to speak all mirth and jest."
Don Pedro laughed, "Being merry suits you best."

Sydney Truelove (age 10)

The Prince gazed after Beatrice as she fled.
"A pleasant-spirited lady," Don Pedro said.
"But she will not consider a husband," he declared.
"She mocks all her suitors," Leonato despaired.
Don Pedro retorted, "We could get a man in her life!
For Benedick, she would make an excellent wife."
Leonato laughed, "Don Pedro, you're a cad.
Married just a week, they would talk themselves mad!"
But now a new scheme simmered in the Prince's mind,
"I will need the help of the three of you combined."
Leonato and Claudio were eager as could be,
And the lady Hero said she would agree.
"We'll start with Benedick," Don Pedro began,
"Come in with me, my friends, and listen to my plan."

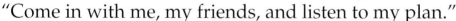

26

Katie Hopkins (age 11)

While Don Pedro's plot was being detailed,
Don John was angry that his scheme had failed.
He snarled, "Claudio's marriage will now proceed."
"Not if I can cross it," Borachio disagreed.
"We'll disgrace Hero. Her servant is the key.
I think I told your lordship, Margaret's fond of me.
I'll convince her to act in a little charade.
She can play Hero in our masquerade.
At her lady's window, she'll stand at my request,
And in the clothes of Hero, Margaret will be dressed.
Her words of love to me will be all part of the plan.
We'll pretend that she has fallen for another man.
With the Prince and Claudio, you'll share Hero's offence,
On the eve of the wedding, they'll observe the evidence.
Believing it is Hero, they'll think she is a cheat."
Don John sneered, "Of course, I'll be discreet!"

Your plan is the perfect fit for our puzzle. Claudio shall be blinded by our lies. The more he thinks, the more he will sink into thick despair. His trust for Hero shall dry up like an old prune. His heart shall fade into an icy shell. A thousand ducats is yours if you succeed!

Don John

Story: Joy McKeown (age 7)
Picture: Andrea Petrak (age 8)

And so the week passed, toward the wedding day,
Benedick strolled in the orchard, his look faraway.
"I wonder that Claudio, a soldier so renowned,
Could fall for the folly of love!" he frowned.
"Affection shall never make me such a fool.
I would not submit to such ridicule!"
Then Don Pedro, Leonato and Claudio, he spied.
"Ha! The Prince and Monsieur Love! I will hide."
For more talk of marriage, he was not keen,
And behind the bushes, he hoped he'd be unseen.

Anika Johnson (age 10)

28

Benedick was unaware he'd already been sighted,
The three men saw him hiding there and were excited.
The Prince spoke loudly and cut to the quick,
"You say your niece loves Signior Benedick?"
Benedick was startled and sat up straight in shock,
He began to quiver and his knees began to knock.
When they glanced towards him, he dropped out of sight.
Claudio whispered, "Bait the hook well, this fish will bite!"
Leonato raised his voice, "Yes, it's Benedick she adores,
Hero says she writes to him and her passion soars.
Twenty times she's up at night, then rips her notes apart,
Knowing how he'd spurn her love and torment her heart."
"I wish she had bestowed this love on me," the Prince replied.
"Benedick should know of her affection," he cried.
Claudio disagreed, "He'd mock her, the old sinner!"
And then the three departed and went in for dinner.

Anika Johnson (age 10)

Benedick rose from hiding, "This can be no trick,
They seem to pity the lady who's lovesick."
He felt his pulse quicken and his face began to burn,
"Beatrice adores me! This love I must return!"
Like a bolt of lightning, everything had changed.
His ideas of marriage were now rearranged.
"I shall be the butt of many jokes, I fear,
For my thoughts on matrimony, I have long made clear.
But shall I let their ridicule deter me?" he implored.
"No, the world must be peopled!" Benedick roared.
"Here comes Beatrice now!" His eyes opened wide.
"I do spy some marks of love in her!" he cried.

I am flabbergasted!
Beatrice loves me! My
mind is bubbling with
joy. This is as wonderful
as chocolate pudding.
She is wise, wealthy,
chatty and beautiful.
What more could a
man want?
                Benedick

Story: Michelle Brandon (age 7)
Picture: Britta Johnson (age 7)

Beatrice spoke coldly, her voice sounding shrill,
"I'm sent to summon you to dinner, against my will."
Benedick beamed, "I thank you for your pains."
Beatrice glared, "I wonder at your brains!
If it had been painful, I would not have come!"
Then she stomped away, looking awfully glum.
"Ha!" laughed Benedick, "I know her techniques,
There's a double meaning in what she speaks.
Her gruff behaviour is transparent as glass,
Our future together shall soon come to pass!"
So Benedick was convinced by the little spoof,
And Beatrice herself had provided the proof.

Dear Diary,
Beatrice has invited me to supper. I saw that twinkle in her eyes and that tiny smile on her face. Romance and love are in the air. My heart dances with excitement. Ooo, life is so good!
                    Benedick

Story: Rhianna More (age 7)
Picture: Elly Vousden (age 8)

Beatrice

Next, it was the ladies' turn to change Beatrice's heart,
Hero and her gentlewomen would each play a part.
"Good Margaret," cried Hero, "run thee to the parlour!
Tell Beatrice that, with Ursula, I gossip in the arbour."
Step one of the plan seemed to work like a breeze,
Beatrice rushed to the orchard and hid behind the trees.
At first, they were whispering so she couldn't hear,
Beatrice crept closer when the coast was clear.

Anika Johnson (age 10)

Ursula was speaking and her words she could not miss,
"My lady, are you sure that Benedick loves Beatrice?"
Hero replied, "So says the Prince and my fiancé.
They begged me to inform Beatrice without delay.
But I warned them that this idea might not be wise,
No man deserves the scorn I'm sure she would devise."
Ursula objected, "You must tell her before long,
To refuse so rare a gentleman as Benedick is wrong."
Hero argued, "So turns she every man the wrong side out.
Beatrice cannot love, of that there is no doubt."
Then they lowered their voices, finished with their scam.
Ursula whispered, "We have caught her, madame."
"If it prove so," said Hero, "then loving goes by haps,
Some Cupid kills with arrows, some with traps."

Dear Ursula,
Yes I'm positive Benedick loves Beatrice.
He's sick with love! Every night he writes
to her, then rips up the page. It's a pity
he doesn't use his energy to tell her
how he feels. But Beatrice is so full of
scorn! No ... his love will melt away
like a burning candle.

Hero

Story: Elizabeth Farrell (age 7)
Picture: Eliza Johnson (age 9)

33

Beatrice was dazed as they disappeared from view,
"What fire is in mine ears? Can this be true?
Stand I condemned for pride and scorn so much?" she cried.
"Could it be that Benedick wants me for his bride?"
The passion in her heart she felt anew,
"Contempt, farewell, and maiden pride, adieu."
Beatrice was overwhelmed by what she had learned,
"Benedick, love on! Your feelings shall be returned!"

Jumping Jackhammers! Have I died and gone to heaven? Benedick has spilled his love on me. This is charming news indeed. And to think, I didn't even know he had a heart!
Beatrice

Story: Sam Johnson (age 7)
Picture: Michelle Stevenson (age 11)

Beatrice

In Leonato's house, there was a jovial atmosphere,
Everyone was excited, as Hero's wedding day drew near.
The sweet smell of perfume wafted through the air.
Claudio teased, "It's from Benedick, I declare.
He cleaned his hat this morning and gone is his beard.
Look at him, Don Pedro, he's acting mighty weird.
The sweet youth's in love!" Claudio insisted.
"I have a toothache!" Benedick resisted.
Then he turned to Leonato, "Sir, will you walk with me?"
As they left, Don Pedro said, "It's about Beatrice, I guarantee!"

Katie Hopkins (age 11)

But the mood of happiness quickly changed to gloom,
When the evil Don John entered the room.
"Count Claudio, I have something to convey,
It may affect your plans with your fiancée.
Though your wedding tomorrow, I do not wish to spoil,
I come to inform you that your lady is disloyal!"
"Who? Hero?" Claudio looked horrified.
"Disloyal? Can this be the truth?" he cried.
"Even she," Don John stated, pretending distress.
"The word is too good to paint out her wickedness.
Come with me tonight and observe her cheat on you.
At her chamber window, you'll see her love's untrue."

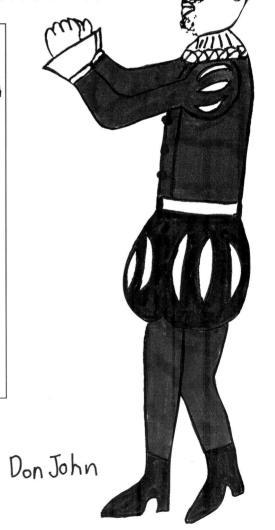

Dear Claudio,
Your lovely lady is a disgrace and a traitor for she has betrayed you for another man. I know you are dumbfounded but I speak the truth. Tonight at Hero's chamber window you will see for yourself. No one should trust her!!
                    Don John

Story: Willie Malmo (age 7)
Picture: Eliza Johnson (age 9)

Don John

36

Claudio turned to the Prince, "Could this be so?"
"I will not think it!" protested Don Pedro.
"If I see anything tonight," Claudio sternly said,
"Tomorrow I'll shame Hero and we will not be wed!"
The Prince agreed with Claudio, "If this is the case,
I will join in proclaiming Hero's disgrace."
Don John stated, "At midnight, you'll see enough."
With that he departed. They'd fallen for the bluff.

Dear Diary,
My soul is crushed! The love and cheer of life turns into screams of pain! A cloud of rage storms upon my mind. Hero's tender lips kiss but not on me! Hero wounds me, but they are wounds you cannot see.
Claudio

Story: Kelsey Cunningham (age 8)
Picture: Kim Brown (age 10)

Now each night in Messina, the police were in pursuit
Of those in the town who were held in disrepute.
Dogberry, the Master Constable, was in charge of his crew,
And demanded of his officers, "Are you good men and true?"
He instructed them at length on their nightly protocol,
As his befuddled group tried to understand it all.
"George Seacole, since you can read and write,
You will lead the watch and bear the lantern tonight.
And, to my fellow constables, try not to offend,
If you meet a thief, this is what I recommend.
The less you get involved, the better you will be,
Let him show himself, then allow him to go free.
Call at all the ale-houses and bid those drunk to bed!
If they will not leave, look the other way instead.
And, honest gentlemen, for my final chore,
Hero's wedding is tomorrow, so guard Leonato's door."

38

Laura Bates (age 10)

And so the night watchmen in the drizzling rain,
Stood quiet as church mice, on guard once again.
It was then they heard Borachio bragging to a friend,
"Conrade, stand closer and you will comprehend.
Hey man," Borachio swaggered, "I put on quite a show!"
He jingled coins in his pocket and swayed to and fro.
"I've been celebrating!" he added with a smirk,
"Don John paid a thousand ducats for my night's work.
And I will, like a true drunkard, utter all to thee."
The watch were now on tiptoes, straining to see.

My pockets are jingling with money. It was like stealing candy from a baby. I tell you (burp) it was a cinch! I just named my price and the thousand ducats were mine! Now listen up, buddy. Let me tell you how it all began...
Borachio

Story: Courtney Cunningham (age 7)
Picture: Sydney Truelove (age 9)

Borachio

"I have tonight wooed Margaret, I knew I would not fail.
Imagine the scene," he burped, as he continued his tale.
"At her lady's window, she answered in Hero's name,
And wearing Hero's clothes was all part of the game.
Now Claudio was watching our little liaison
Along with the Prince and my master, Don John.
Away rushed Claudio, enraged beyond belief.
Tomorrow," he smirked, "the wedding will be brief.
When it's time to share their sacred vows at church,
Claudio will shame Hero and leave her in the lurch!"

Cagney Schaeffer (age 11)

Just then a loud voice bellowed in protest,
"We charge you in the Prince's name. You're under arrest!"
The officers had heard Borachio's every word.
They were honest fellows and would not be deterred.
The first watchman shouted, "Call up, Dogberry!
We know a pair of villains! This is lechery!"
"Masters, masters," Conrade tried to explain the fuss.
The second watchman cried, "Do not speak. Come with us!"

What is it they're saying? Margaret... Hero... leaning out of windows...pretending... Claudio... shaming Hero...Why this is the most despicable deed in police history. We must stop these villains! Men, on the count of three, "POLICE! YOU'RE UNDER ARREST!"

Story: Emily Dunbar (age 8)
Picture: Théa Pel (age 8)

41

The day of the wedding dawned bright and clear,
Everyone was happy and bustling with good cheer.
Margaret and Beatrice were admiring Hero's gown,
When Ursula rushed in, her face twisted with a frown.
"I hope you know it's getting late and Claudio's inside,
He comes with his friends to fetch the waiting bride."
In the next room Hero's father was busy too,
When Dogberry and his partner arrived for an interview.
They came to inform him of two villains they'd arrested,
But chattered on so long that Leonato protested,
"I am now in great haste. You said you would be brief.
Examine them yourselves." Then he fled in relief.

Leonato

To Dogberry,
Get to the point Master Constable! I don't have all day. Claudio and Hero are to be married this afternoon. Tables need to be set, flowers ordered, banners hung and the food tested. I am a very busy man and have no time for your problems.
                    Leonato

Story: Jessica Finck (age 7)
Picture: Robyn Lafontaine (age 10)

42

As the hour drew near, the townsfolk gathered in delight,
Hero, looking radiant, was a beautiful sight.
Her dress was magnificent. Everyone was impressed.
They sighed with pleasure at this union to be blessed.
"Come, Friar Francis," said Leonato, looking proud,
"Begin the ceremony," and he smiled at the crowd.
This was a precious moment in his daughter's life,
Very soon the two would be husband and wife.
The Friar asked Claudio, "Do you agree?
Have you come, my lord, to marry this lady?"

Robyn Lafontaine (age 10)

43

Hero trembled with excitement, her eyes were aglow.
Claudio stared at her and firmly answered, "No!"
Hero gasped in horror and began to shake.
Leonato cried, "Friar, there must be some mistake!
Claudio is playing with the words that you spoke."
But Hero's father wondered if it really was a joke!
The priest continued, though he too was aghast,
"Hero, do you take Claudio for your husband?" he asked.

Eliza Johnson (age 10)

"I do!" Hero promised, her voice loud and clear.
Claudio turned to her father with an angry sneer,
"Will you with free and unconstrained soul, give me this maid?"
"As freely, son, as God did give her me," he conveyed.
"Then take her back again," Claudio fumed.
He pushed Hero away, "Our wedding is doomed!
Her blush is guiltiness, not modesty!" he roared.
Leonato was dazed, "What do you mean, my lord?"
"This looks not like a nuptial!" Benedick said.
"What's wrong with you, Claudio?" Hero cried in dread.
"What man was he last night at your window," he retorted,
"Between twelve and one, with whom you consorted?"

45

"I talked with no man at that hour!" Hero implored.
Don Pedro interrupted, "That's a lie!" he roared,
"At your chamber window, in the moonlight,
I heard you speak words of love to a man last night."
Claudio cried, "Hero, most foul, most fair, farewell!"
His cruel words to her sounded like a death knell.
Hero tried to speak, but could not make a sound,
She staggered, then slumped upon the ground.
Claudio gazed at her but had no sympathy,
Then left with Don Pedro, so angry was he.

Dear Diary,
Today was shocking! The wedding was going fine until the "I do" part. Then Claudio erupted, his eyes red as fire! You should have seen the congregation. They all sat with their mouths open. Claudio must have got up on the wrong side of the bed! The wedding was a catastrophe!

A guest at the wedding

Story: Elizabeth Farrell (age 8)
Picture: Elly Vousden (age 8)

Beatrice rushed to her dear cousin's side,
"Hero is dead, I think!" she mournfully cried.
"Help, Uncle!" she wailed, "This is so unjust!"
In her cousin's honour she had never lost trust.
But Hero's father believed the evidence,
And would not speak in his daughter's defence.
Leonato raged, "Hero is to blame,
Death is the fairest cover for her shame.
Do not live, Hero!" His fury intensified.
"On my soul," moaned Beatrice, "my cousin is belied."
But Hero's eyelids flickered and life was restored,
"Have comfort, lady," Friar Francis implored.
Hero vowed, "Friar, if any man with me conversed,
Then, refuse me, hate me, let me be cursed!"

THE MESSINA PRESS

CLAUDIO DUMPS HERO
Reporter: Lauri-Beth Lewis

Friday, April 24 Claudio was to marry the fair Hero. When the young Count was asked, he angrily yelled, "NO!" Hero trembled with dread. Claudio hollered, "Your fear is guilt!" The audience gasped as Hero dropped to the ground in shock. Was it fear or guilt that made Hero faint? The answer will appear in further editions of the Messina Press.

Story: Lauri-Beth Lewis (age 7)
Picture: Anika Johnson (age 10)

47

For a time the Friar had been observing the accused,
"Leonato, hear me, your daughter's been misused!
This sweet and gentle lady is innocent, Your Grace.
Pause awhile and let my counsel sway you in this case.
I have a plan that will in due course,
On Hero's behalf, change slander to remorse.
Let it be known through Messina, that Hero has died,
And that Claudio's accusations killed his bride.
On her family's tomb hang a mournful epitaph,
Stage a mock burial and grieve on her behalf.
In life, we value more what we can't possess,
Claudio will be sorry and feel great distress.
In the end," the Friar smiled, "I have no doubt,
Hero's name will be cleared and the truth will out."
Then he turned to Hero, "Endure, and patience give."
He held out his hand, "Come, lady, die to live!"

Dear Hero,
Do not fret, my lady. Here is my
secret plan. Your father will spread
the news that you have died of
sorrow. Claudio will be heart-
broken and gladly apologize
to the citizens of Messina.
Will we catch this fish with
our bait? Only time will tell!
                    The Friar

Story: Elizabeth Farrell (age 8)
Picture: Anika Johnson (age 10)

As the Friar led Leonato and Hero away,
Beatrice and Benedick were left alone that day.
Benedick was gentle with the lady, for whom he longed,
"Surely, I do believe your fair cousin is wronged."
Beatrice was weeping, "Hero speaks the truth,
How much I would owe to the man who offers proof!"
Benedick drew closer to the lady he admired,
"Is there any way to show such friendship?" he inquired,
"For I do love nothing in the world so well as you!
Beatrice, by my sword, I believe you love me too."

Katie Hopkins (age 11)

And, though it took some prodding, Beatrice finally confessed,
"I love you with so much of my heart that none is left to protest."
Benedick smiled "I'd do anything you commanded."
"Kill Claudio!" Beatrice firmly demanded.
"Not for the wide world!" he bellowed, astounded.
"You kill me to deny it! Claudio's proof is unfounded.
Sweet Hero, she is wronged, she is slandered, she is undone."
Benedick tried to stop her, as she turned to run.
"Enough!" exclaimed Benedick, his face looking grim.
"I am engaged!" he cried, "I will challenge him!"

Katie Hopkins (age 11)

Now throughout Messina, the sad news quickly spread
That Leonato's daughter, the Lady Hero, was dead.
In the city's jail, the hour was getting late
As Borachio and Conrade awaited their fate.
For the interview by Dogberry seemed to take all day,
The Town Clerk interrupted wanting to have his say.
"Master Constable, let's get to the offence.
Call forth the watch to present the evidence."
And so the sordid details were finally related,
The clerk who was recording them became agitated.
"Let these men be bound and brought to Leonato's place.
The Governor must be informed. This is a disgrace!"

Anika Johnson (age 10)

Meanwhile, Signior Leonato ached with grief.
Nothing could bring him comfort and relief.
The Friar had convinced him Hero was not to blame,
And now her stricken father was filled with shame.
Just then Don Pedro and Claudio drew nigh,
The old man raised his sword with a battle cry.
"Thou hast so wronged mine innocent child and me,
I am forced to ignore my age, and challenge thee!"
Then Antonio, his brother, jumped into the fray,
"God knows I loved my niece, and you shall pay."
"Away!" shouted Claudio, his honour offended.
The Prince added, "Let this argument be ended."

Story: Emily Dunbar (age 8)
Picture: Caitlin Ellison (age 9)

Oh Hero, my Hero, my mind is wailing in grief.
How could I have been so harsh? I'm so
sorry for the cruel words I spoke. I
am just an old fool and I was wrong.
Claudio is the one who should be shamed.
Let the combat begin!

Leonato

As Leonato and Antonio withdrew,
Signior Benedick strode quickly into view.
Don Pedro joked, "You almost parted a fight.
With two old men it would have been quite a sight!"
Benedick's face took on a sickly pallor,
"In a false quarrel there is no true valour!
You have, among you, an innocent life shed,
And your brother, Don John, from Messina has fled.
Claudio, our dispute is long overdue,
You are a villain and I challenge you!
Meet me when you dare!" Then he stormed away.
"He is in earnest!" cried Don Pedro in dismay.

To Claudio and Don Pedro,
You villains have killed
a sweet lady. Both of you
are disgraceful cowards!
In the name of Leonato,
I challenge you to
risk your blood. Hero
deserved better!
                Benedick

Story: Max Besworth (age 8)
Picture: Elizabeth Farrell (age 8)

Benedick

At that moment, a parade of men drew near,
Why two were in chains was not at first clear.
Don Pedro was stunned, "This makes no sense.
My brother's men bound? What's their offence?"
Constable Dogberry replied in a manner grand,
But, as usual, his explanation was hard to understand.
So the Prince appealed to Borachio instead,
But what he had to say filled Don Pedro with dread.
Borachio was contrite and answered on bended knee,
"Sweet Prince, listen, and let this Count kill me.
It was Margaret at the window," Borachio cried,
"It was a shameful trick. Fair Hero never lied!"
Then he admitted everything to the last detail,
"The lady is dead, upon mine and my master's betrayal!"

Sydney Truelove (age 10)

54

Claudio shuddered and his heart began to race,
A look of horror spread across Don Pedro's face.
The words of the confession rushed upon him like a flood,
"Claudio, runs not this speech, like iron through your blood?"
"It's as though I drank poison while he spoke," he replied.
And for the first time Claudio saw the error of his pride.
To his sweet Hero, he'd been so heartless and unjust,
His ego and his honour had overwhelmed his trust.

What have I done? My heart is burning my soul and my life, for I have destroyed my love with false words. I am so dreadfully sorry. I will never forgive myself!

Claudio

Story: Sam Johnson (age 7)
Picture: Sydney Truelove (age 10)

Claudio

Leonato and his brother returned into view,
The Town Clerk had revealed the facts, now proven true.
Hero's father demanded, "Which is the one, I despise?
Come now," he shouted angrily, "let me see his eyes!"
Borachio was repentant, "I do not disagree,
If you would know your wronger, look on me!"
Leonato charged, "You killed my innocent child!"
"Yes, I alone," Borachio cried, "I should be reviled."
"No, not so, villain!" Leonato exclaimed,
"Claudio and Don Pedro also must be blamed.
I will thank you all, until my final breath,
You are responsible for my daughter's death."

You have destroyed my most precious possession. My daughter was as innocent as a lamb and as gentle as a spring rain. You have wasted a beautiful soul. There will never be another Hero!
Leonato

Story: Rhianna More (age 7)
Picture: Ewan Dunbar (age 8)

Leonato

56

Claudio cried, "Choose your revenge for my cure,
Whatever penance you decide, I will endure!"
Don Pedro exclaimed, "Accept my guilt, too.
By my soul, how can I make amends to you?"
"Proclaim my daughter's innocence," Leonato replied,
"Let the people know the truth of how she died.
Hang her an epitaph upon her tomb tonight,
And pay your respects at the burial site.
Tomorrow morning to my house direct your feet,
The daughter of my brother, I want you to meet.
She is almost the copy of my dead child,
Marry her Claudio and I'll be reconciled."
Claudio vowed, "To your merciful offer, I agree,
Your overkindness doth wring tears from me!"

Hero was a living song. She brightened the city of Messina even on the gloomiest days. But now I stop to sigh. My only love is gone, gone like the wind. Hero, if you can hear me now, I beg forgiveness!
Claudio

Story: Elizabeth Farrell (age 8)
Picture: Caitlin Ellison (age 9)

And so that evening, on Hero's behalf,
Claudio delivered a touching epitaph.
Then he hung the scroll and bid her goodnight,
Promising yearly to repeat this rite.
The hours passed, as hymns were played,
And tears were shed for their Hero betrayed.
Don Pedro sighed, "Look, the gentle day,
Dapples the drowsy east with spots of grey.
Come, Claudio, you must make a fresh start,
To Leonato's home we must depart."

Eliza Johnson (age 10)

Meanwhile, Leonato's joy could not be denied,
And his daughter once again filled him with pride.
Antonio smiled, "It all worked out so fine!"
Then Leonato shared the last of his design.
"My dear daughter and you gentlewomen all,
Withdraw and return veiled when I call."
As the ladies departed, he continued to advise,
"Antonio, you will present my Hero in disguise.
He'll believe it is your daughter," he added with a grin.
"Everything is ready! Within the hour, we'll begin!"
Benedick interrupted, "But I need a helping hand,
To bind me, or undo me, do you understand?"
Leonato asked, "And what is your desire?"
"To marry Beatrice," he replied, "the lady I admire."
"My heart is with your liking!" Leonato agreed,
The Friar nodded, "A double wedding will proceed."

Leonato

Dear Leonato,
The flower of love has bloomed
and Beatrice is the rosiest of
all. The world awakens under
her feet. If I can't have her
hand in marriage, my dreams
shall evaporate like early
morning dew. It's your decision.
Light a candle or snuff it!
                    Benedick

Story: Joy McKeown (age 7)
Picture: Valerie Sproat (age 11)

59

Then Claudio arrived with Don Pedro by his side,
Leonato looked serious and dignified.
He inquired of the Count, "Are you resolved to wed?"
"My will is absolute!" Claudio promptly said.
It was then that the ladies appeared on cue,
Behind veils, their faces hidden from view.
Claudio wondered, "Which one's to be my bride?"
"It will be my daughter," Antonio replied.
Then Hero stepped forward in her disguise,
A questioning look was in her eyes.
"Please, let me see your face!" Claudio pleaded,
"No, not yet!" Leonato quickly interceded.
"That you shall not till you take her hand,
And promise to marry her, as we planned."
Claudio knelt before her and delivered his plea,
"I am your husband if you like of me."

Hero

My hands grip my mask as tight as a boa constrictor wrapping its prey. I desperately want to reveal myself and shout, "HALLELUJAH WORLD! I AM THE REAL HERO!" I forgive Claudio for all the troubled times but feel redeemed with new hope and dreams.

Hero

Story: Jessica Finck (age 7)
Picture: Robyn Lafontaine (age 10)

60

Leonato's daughter slowly raised her veil,
Revealing her face and every beautiful detail.
"Another Hero!" Claudio gasped in delight.
He was amazed by this wonderous sight.
"The former Hero!" cried Don Pedro, "Hero that is dead!"
"She died only while her slander lived," Leonato said.
"All will be explained," added the Friar delighted,
"But now to the chapel so these two can be united."

As I bustled to the church, a voice from So far yet so near seemed to whisper, "Today will shape the rest of your life!" I peered at the masked lady and then I took her hand. When she lowered her mask I gasped a muffled breath for this was the true Hero! She stood smiling and warm and I read in her eyes, "I'll love you in spite of your faults." Leonato was a river of tears. I was filled with raging affection!
                              Claudio

Story: Kelsey Cunningham (age 8)
Picture: Robyn Lafontaine (age 10)

Hero

61

"Pardon me," cried Benedick, "but something is amiss."
He surveyed the other ladies, "Which one is Beatrice?"
"I answer to that name. What is your will?"
Benedick inquired, "Do not you love me still?"
"Why, no, no more than reason," she cried as she unveiled,
"Benedick, do not you love me?" Beatrice wailed.
"Truly, no, no more than reason," Benedick's mind was a blur.
"Nonsense!" cried Claudio, "Here's a sonnet you wrote to her!"
Hero interrupted, "Beatrice penned one too!
She calls him her wildest dream come true!"
"Our own hands against our hearts!" Benedick laughed in bliss,
Then they sealed their love with a tender kiss!
Benedick grinned, "Don Pedro, you need a new lease on life."
Then he tipped his hat, "Get a wife, I say, get a wife!"

All our lives we've traded insults and they have bounced back and forth faster than a great ball of fire. But now our words will stay wrapped in the sweet blanket of love.
    Beatrice and Benedick

Story: Joy McKeown (age 7)
Picture: Ashley Kropf (age 10)

Now, Beatrice vows she wed to save Benedick's life.
Benedick says he tied the knot to take pity on his wife.
And though it wasn't nothing, and there was much ado,
My tale ends on a cheerful note. My friends, I bow to you.

63

Katie Hopkins (age 11)

Parents and Educators

This book can be used for a variety of activities, either at home or in the classroom. Here are a few suggestions you might find helpful.

- Locate Messina, Sicily, on a map of the world.
- Find the distance from Messina to Padua and Florence in Italy.
- Assemble a glossary of words from the play (for example, threescore, arbour, ducats, epitaph)
- Choreograph a dance and compose music for the party welcoming the soldiers back from war.
- Design and create masks for Benedick, Beatrice and the guests at the celebration.
- Create and decorate menus for the party, using food that would have been eaten during Elizabethan times.
- Write a diary for Benedick and Beatrice, adding to it daily.
- Create a tableau (a 'frozen picture') of a particular scene.
- Develop a timeline for the events.
- Publish newspaper accounts of the wedding of Hero and Claudio. Add reports of other news events in Messina.
- Draft an advice column for the characters in the play and include responses in the newspaper.

Educators who wish to stage performances of *Much Ado About Nothing for Kids* should contact the author to request permission:
Fax: (519) 273-0712
E-mail: lburdett@shakespearecanbefun.com

Anika Johnson (age 7)

Front cover: Elly Vousden (age 8)
Title page: Anika Johnson (age 9)
Back cover story: Paul McGarry (age 7)
Back cover picture: Victoria Visser (age 7)

Other books in the series:

A Child's Portrait of Shakespeare
Twelfth Night for Kids
Macbeth for Kids
A Midsummer Night's Dream for Kids
Romeo and Juliet for Kids
The Tempest for Kids
Hamlet for Kids